BREAKFASTLOVE

David Bez of Salad Pride

BREAKFASTLOVE

Perfect little bowls of quick, healthy breakfasts

QUADRILLE.

This book is dedicated to my mum, my wife and my son.

Publishing Director: Sarah Lavelle
Creative Director: Helen Lewis
Senior Editor: Céline Hughes
Designer and Photographer: David Bez
Production: Tom Moore, Vincent Smith

First published in 2016 by
Quadrille Publishing
Pentagon House
52–54 Southwark Street
London SE1 1UN
www.quadrille.co.uk

Quadrille is an imprint of Hardie Grant
www.hardiegrant.com.au

Cataloguing in Publication Data: a catalogue record for this
book is available from the British Library.

ISBN: 978 184949 714 5

Printed in China

10 9 8 7 6 5 4 3 2 1

Contents

The need for a better breakfast

How often do we eat breakfast, not really thinking about it properly?

Looking back on the breakfasts I've eaten throughout my life, I had milk and cookies up to the age of 15, then cappuccino and croissants until just a couple of years ago.

After re-thinking how to have lunch in the workplace a few years ago and launching my first book, *Salad Love*, I thought it was important to apply the same principles and attitude to what's commonly considered the most important meal of the day. A good breakfast propels you towards the day and the challenges ahead. I've asked many nutritionists and read many books and articles about what constitutes the best and healthiest breakfast. I've taken that research and, as always, I've gone through my own journey, experimenting on myself, my body and my palate, every day for a good two years.

During this time, I've learned that the food you eat needs to be tantalizing and colourful in order to appeal to your eyes and your imagination. This is Rule Number One. Rule Number Two is to try to use ingredients that are unrefined or as close to their natural state as possible. That's why I say "no" to industrial granolas, flavoured yogurts and overly-processed cereals. I sometimes use cereals, including cornflakes, but I always try to buy the gluten-free and sugar-free versions, and those that are high in fibre.

I've always been very reticent about eating fruit – don't ask me why! I've probably just been lazy about needing to wash or peel them and therefore I've tended to go for an easier, ready-to-eat carb/sugary option. But on my mission to re-educate myself about breakfast, I forced myself to rediscover fruits, one by one, and it's been great. I love them so much now; how could I have gone without them for so long!

I made it my mission to uncover what's generally considered healthy, what the current top nutritionists believe (which might change in a few years…), and I tried to create a common sense, or common ground, that feels true and right and not just trendy.

I also decided to see what various cultures around the world eat for breakfast and I tried to adapt it to my tastes and my culture. I made the decision to explore vegetables and savoury plates in my breakfast, too. From my Italian point of view, breakfast is a sweet affair, but I was surprised to discover that not only do the British have a big tradition of savoury breakfast in the form of fry-ups, but in Asia, South America, Africa, Germany and other parts of Europe there are also plenty of examples of savoury breakfast.

Another basic rule for me is speed. This is not a book about long and luscious Sunday brunches. This book is about everyday breakfasts: easy and quick to prepare at home or even in the kitchen of your office.

There is some pre-prepared stuff (e.g. soaked nuts, seeds and oats, cooked rice and a few blended ingredients), but a little DIY makes things interesting! Often all it takes is a few moments of preparation the night before and by the time you wake up the next morning, you're ready to put your breakfast bowl together. The truth is that a lot of the breakfast products you buy in the supermarket are over-processed and full of sugar.

Mostly, I've always asked the same question about my meals, and breakfast is no exception. Does it taste good? Is it healthy (in a common-sense way)? Does it feel good? Is it easy to make? Is it satisfying? Is it light? Does it weigh you down, or does it fuel and nurture your morning? Does it look good?

I hope I have answered most of them.

Enjoy the journey.

1. Fruit or vegetable

2. Fruit or vegetable

3. Cereal

4. Protein

5. Toppings

6. "Dressing"

Anatomy of a breakfast

When composing my breakfast, I divide it into different layers: fruit and/or vegetables, cereals, proteins, extra toppings and some kind of liquid or "dressing". These are the main ingredients, but as you will see, I often mess around with the formula. It's really up to you to choose what you want to put in it and to enjoy what you are eating.

Fruits and vegetables

The biggest part of my breakfast is the fruit and veg. At least two fruit or veg portions – not cereals – make up the base of my breakfast bowl. This is a big change from conventional breakfasts, in which a big bowl of porridge might be topped with a couple of strawberries. Instead, I have a big dose of fruits and veggies accompanied by some protein and a bit of cereal.

Cereals, grains and seeds

Cereals like oats, cornflakes and quinoa are still part of my diet, but in a much smaller proportion compared to the past. I use around ⅓ cup of (if possible) gluten-free and sugar-free grains.

Protein

You might like to add some protein to your bowl, such as ham, beef or chicken; eggs, fish, yogurt, cheese or tofu; lentils, quinoa, nuts or seeds – depending on your dietary requirements and your taste.

Toppings

Extra toppings can boost the flavours and colours of your breakfast bowl. Try fresh herbs, edible flowers, bee pollen or dried fruits (but no more than a teaspoon of those).

"Dressing"

Then, to top it all off, is the "dressing", or the creamy/liquid part of your breakfast. This can range from juices to dairy and non-dairy milks.

There is a fine balance between all the ingredients; their sweetness or sourness, the size of the pieces, the juiciness of the fruit and vegetables, the crunchiness of the cereals and the nuts, the smoothness and the richness of the dressing.

1. Fruits

Fruits and vegetables should make up more than half of your breakfast, not just because you should eat at least five portions a day to get a range of vitamins, minerals and fibres, but because they are tasty, filling and full of colour.

I favour bigger pieces of fruit over finely chopped ones, so that I can make out every single ingredient properly. For similar reasons, I prefer to keep my fruits raw, as the flavours are more intense that way and the nutritional values are higher. I do, however, occasionally like to add dried fruit, which I'll talk about more on page 23.

The first half of the book is the sweet chapter in which fruits are the heroes, but you'll also spot some fruits in the savoury chapter. There are usually at least four recipes for each of these lovely fruits: apple, apricot, avocado, banana, blueberries, blackberries, cherries, coconut, fig, grape, grapefruit, kiwi, lychee, mango, melon, nectarine, orange, clementine, papaya, passion fruit, physalis, pear, persimmon, pineapple, plum, pomegranate, raspberries, strawberries and watermelon.

I've explored every single fruit thoroughly, every day for at least a week, to make sure that I find the best flavour combinations. As a result, I've fallen in love with fruit again. It's sweet, juicy, flavourful – and so good for me!

2. Vegetables

Vegetables for breakfast? Why not! Do you know that the Turkish eat olives, tomatoes and cucumber for breakfast? The Mexicans might have avocado, tomatoes and peppers with their eggs. So I asked myself, why not use cucumbers, raw or roasted [bell] peppers, carrots, raw or roasted courgettes [zucchini], steamed green beans, roasted butternut squash and aubergines [eggplant] in my breakfast bowl?

Of course, some of these need to be cooked the night before, but this can be as simple as roasting more veg than you need for dinner, or steaming some beans at the same time as you're preparing tomorrow's lunch. I personally like to roast a big batch of veggies and store them in an airtight container in the fridge for a couple of days, ready to go into my breakfast.

3. Cereal

When I was young, I had to have wheat in some form in the morning, with milk of course. Croissants, cookies, any type of bread, possibly toasted; on holiday I might have butter and jam on toast.

I've learned to tame my carb and sugar intake in order to control my sugar rush. I've tried to reduce my carbs while still ingesting just enough to keep me going; just as importantly, I've adapted the variety and quality of my chosen carbs to get more out of them. So, no more white flour or white sugar, but yes to corn, rice, buckwheat, amaranth, quinoa, oats, barley, whole grains, and so on. I always check the sugar content in my pre-prepared breakfast cereals and if you search hard enough you'll find several sugar-free options for cornflakes, bran flakes and even new products like raw granola and muesli containing no refined sugar.

It seems that a bowl of porridge in the morning is a British classic, along with fry-ups and beans on toast. I've never been a big fan of porridge, but I've learned how to like it and use it. The rule is easy: 1 part oats to 2 parts liquid (such as dairy milk, almond milk or water). Place them in a saucepan over a low heat and cook, stirring occasionally, for 8 minutes or until thickened. (Porridge made from amaranth or buckwheat should be cooked for 15 minutes, quinoa for 20 minutes, and rice for 30 minutes.) Sometimes I like to add just a touch of spice to pep things up. I don't usually want more than ⅓ cup porridge, as I prefer the fruits to be the real protagonists in my breakfast.

Soaked oats

Soaking oats overnight makes them substantially more digestible and nutritious, as it helps to break down toxins while keeping them raw. What I enjoy most about a bowl of soaked oats in the morning is that it fills me up all the way until lunchtime. It's no effort at all, but you do have to remember to put the oats on to soak before going to bed the night before. I like to soak them in almond milk, but other options include yogurt, orange juice and apple juice. The rule is easy: 1 part oats to 1 part liquid. Sometimes I add some spice to give it a bit of sparkle, just 1 teaspoon of, for example, cocoa powder, or dried ground cinnamon, maca, açai, lucuma or turmeric.

Granola

A granola is commonly a mixture of grains, dried fruits, nuts and seeds baked together with a sweetener and an oil. Everyone makes theirs slightly differently, switching the types of ingredients for what they have to hand.

Most storebought granolas are full of cheap or refined oils (sunflower or palm) and cheap or refined sweeteners (like white sugar or golden syrup). The only way to really trust a granola is to make it with your own hands in your own kitchen so that you are in control of the sugar content and the taste.

I'm not a big fan of granolas containing too many different grains, fruits, nuts and seeds. I quite like to see what I'm eating and identify the different tastes. So for me, the perfect combination is just one grain, one dried fruit, one nut or seed and maybe one spice – but you don't have to be as minimalist as me.

I like to use natural sweeteners as much as I can. Honey is good, but it's such a shame to bake it, as it loses all its antibacterial properties in the process.

I also like to use "grains" like buckwheat or quinoa (both actually "pseudocereals"). They need to be soaked overnight in water before baking. For a sweetener, I like to use pineapple or apple juice (sometimes even carrot or beetroot juice), and coconut oil as my oil of choice. This is my favourite recipe: preheat the oven to 160°C/325°F; on a non-stick baking sheet, mix together 1 cup rolled oats, ½ cup fruit juice, 1 tbsp nuts or seeds (walnuts, hazelnuts, cashew nuts, sunflower seeds, pumpkin seeds), 1 tbsp dried fruit (coconut shavings, apricots, dates, raisins, mango, pineapple, goji berries), 1 tbsp coconut oil and 1 tsp spice (see opposite); spread out in a single layer and bake for at least 30 minutes until golden, stirring occasionally.

4. Protein

One part of your breakfast must be a protein. I'm sure you know by now that you can get proteins from a wide range of sources, not just meat and fish.

From nuts to yogurts, eggs to cheese, ham to fish – there are plenty of ways to fulfill your protein intake early in the day. It will fill you up and give you energy all morning. Of course, nuts and seeds pair so naturally with fruits, but I love to experiment with cheese and salty meats like ham alongside fruits. (I sometimes put cheese in vegetarian salads because some vegetarians choose to eat cheese, and because there is a growing number of rennet-free cheeses available, but do replace them if necessary.) Fish and the other meats mostly make savoury bowls, but be prepared for a couple of surprises. As well as cheese, savoury protein options can include pulses like lentils, chickpeas [garbanzo beans], hummus and beans.

In my research I have found that the most typical feature of breakfasts around the world is egg – be it England, America, Spain, Japan, France, Brazil, Egypt, Mexico, Germany, Israel or Korea. So if in doubt, add a poached, fried, hard- or soft-boiled egg, or an omelette to your breakfast bowl.

5. Toppings

These are all the herby and sweet ingredients that you need just a tablespoon or two of to really lift your breakfast. I like dried fruits, such as apricots, dates, raisins, prunes, blueberries, coconut, mango, pineapple, mulberries and goji berries. I put bee pollen in this category even though it's not a dried fruit, because it enhances the sweet accent of the breakfast. I don't put dried fruit in the same category as fresh fruit since their sugar content (and flavour) is so intense that just a tablespoon of them is enough.

In savoury breakfasts, a handful of fresh herbs provide a fragrant note. I favour basil, chives, coriander (cilantro), dill, mint, oregano, parsley, rosemary, sage, tarragon and thyme. Mint and tarragon even work in sweet recipes!

6. "Dressing"

A little dressing in your bowl goes a long way to bringing all the elements together. It completes your breakfast; without it, the bowl would seem dry, disjointed and sad, almost inedible in fact. Even milk doesn't make your breakfast stand out very much, so I play around with all sorts of alternatives.

All your dressings should be a balance of sweet richness (from oil or nuts), sourness (lemon) and a bit of spice (ginger, cocoa, cinnamon, cardamom, turmeric, maca, even salt and chilli), and should meld into something creamy rather than too runny and smooth. Natural yogurt is the perfect candidate. I never use flavoured yogurt, which is often loaded with sugar, but I do add some flavourings and I've even tried to create my own alternatives to yogurt. There are plenty of dairy-free yogurts on the market now, from the soy ones (not my favourite – I don't like the taste and soy is still a controversial ingredient) to the coconut ones. Non-dairy creams range from oat to almond, or you can make your own version (see page 29).

If your bowl already features porridge or soaked oats, there is no need for extra liquid.

In the savoury chapter, I mostly stick to a drizzle of oil to dress my breakfast, but once in a while, I go a bit more funky with hummus or Avocado Mash (see page 27).

Banana and lemon mash

This is an unusual, raw substitute for classic yogurt and I love it. It's a true nutrient bomb.

Mash together 1 banana with the juice of ½ lemon. Jazz it up, if you like, with 1 teaspoon ground spice like ginger or turmeric and you'll feel the kick. Orange or grapefruit juice can replace lemon juice, but avoid sweet juices as banana is very sweet by itself. Very occasionally, I use almond or coconut milk.

Avocado mash

Another alternative to yogurt, this is my take on guacamole and best used in savoury bowls. It works well as a creamy "dressing" but unlike guacamole, it doesn't have any flavourings like garlic, onion, chilli or salt.

Mash together 1 ripe avocado with the juice of ½ lemon. Orange or apple juice can replace lemon juice. Jazz it up, if you like, with 1 teaspoon ground spice like ginger, turmeric or even cocoa powder (which works very well with orange juice in sweet bowls). If you want it sweeter, you can add 1 tablespoon honey (preferably raw).

Nut "yogurts" and "creams"

I've been looking for a raw alternative to dairy yogurt for a long time. Coconut yogurt from supermarkets is lovely, but eventually I found a winner: it turns out that nuts and seeds are the perfect raw protein alternative to dairy. Blend together 1 cup nuts or seeds, 1 cup water and a drizzle of lemon juice and you'll have a new kind of yogurt. The nuts blend better if they have been soaked in water overnight. The best texture is achieved with cashew nuts, which produce a sweet and unctuous consistency – just perfect.

If you want to flavour your homemade yogurt, add a handful of fresh fruit and maybe 1 teaspoon honey (preferably raw) to the blender. I've had great results with blueberries, strawberries, pineapple, mango, figs, apricots and nectarines.

You can be creative and get a creamier, more dessert-like "cream" by replacing the lemon juice with spice and honey. Blend together 1 cup nuts or seeds, 1 cup water, 1 teaspoon spice (like cocoa powder, ground ginger, ground cinnamon, lavender or vanilla extract) and 1 teaspoon honey (preferably raw).

Better breakfasts

For the past two years, I've tested the boundaries of a good morning meal. As expected, I had to reject a lot of my experiments due to poor flavour combinations or ill-judged proportions. I'm so happy I did this research because I've made countless great discoveries and found new ways to take care of myself. I love all veggies even more than I used to, but the real revelation has been how much I love fruit. Sour, sweet, rich, creamy, tasty, vibrant, fresh and nutritious, fruits are the ultimate bounty of the natural world, the quintessentially perfect food.

Gradually my sugar cravings have subsided and any cravings I have are more likely for natural rather than refined white sugars – which is much more manageable and less fattening. I'm not saying that eating these breakfasts will help you lose weight – I can't promise that – but I didn't start this journey in order to lose weight and I don't even own bathroom scales any more. What I am sure of is how much I've enjoyed all these breakfasts – the textures, colours and flavours – and how valuable it's been to figure out what's good and bad for my body first thing in the morning. Now I know how to prepare ingredients in the most natural, healthy and tasty way possible.

I believe that health starts from within us, from the way we feel and the way we view food. Attitude is everything. In turn, the nutrients found in the food we consume affects our mood and our wellbeing. Everything is connected. If we eat happy, beautiful, healthy and nutritious food, we are more likely to be happy, healthy, gorgeous and satisfied; our mood will lift and we will flourish.

I feel nourished and nurtured now. I didn't feel that way when I was eating pastries and sweet treats every morning for years; my blood sugar levels frequently spiked and I had to feed my desire for sugars throughout the day, from morning to late night.

While setting myself the breakfast challenge, I also started taking more exercise, especially cycling. Weaning myself off white sugars made me more active and less inclined to laziness. As I've said, everything in body and mind is connected.

I wrote *Breakfast Love* to inspire you to start a new journey towards a better way of eating and a better life, starting from the first and most important meal of the day.

Take care.

Sweet

Strawberries, Apple, Chia & Poppy Seeds

INGREDIENTS

½ tsp chia seeds, soaked overnight in ⅓ cup almond milk
handful of strawberries, chopped
1 apple, chopped
1 tsp poppy seeds

VEGETARIAN ALTERNATIVE

Replace the soaked chia seeds with some classic (dairy) milk porridge

Apricot, Blueberries, Oats & Sesame Seeds

INGREDIENTS

⅓ cup oats, soaked overnight in ⅓ cup almond milk
2 apricots, chopped
handful of blueberries
1 tbsp sesame seeds

VEGETARIAN
SAVOURY ALTERNATIVE
*Add 30 g [1 oz]
goat cheese and replace
the soaked oats with
(water) porridge*

Strawberries, Passion Fruit, Cereal & Cashews

INGREDIENTS

handful of gluten-free cereal flakes
handful of strawberries, chopped
⅓ cup Cashew "Yogurt" flavoured with strawberries
    (page 29)
handful of cashew nuts
seeds from 1 passion fruit

VEGETARIAN ALTERNATIVE

Replace the Cashew "Yogurt" with dairy strawberry yogurt

Cherries, Nectarine, Porridge & Hemp Seeds

INGREDIENTS

⅓ cup porridge made with rice milk (page 16)
1 nectarine, sliced
handful of cherries, pitted and halved
2 tbsp natural yogurt
1 tbsp shelled hemp seeds

VEGAN ALTERNATIVE
Replace the natural yogurt with coconut yogurt or Cashew "Yogurt" (page 29)

Strawberries, Pineapple, Buckwheat & Yogurt

INGREDIENTS

⅓ cup natural yogurt
1 small wedge of pineapple, chopped
handful of strawberries, chopped
50 g [⅓ cup] buckwheat, cooked
1 tbsp pumpkin seeds
handful of fresh mint, torn

VEGAN ALTERNATIVE

Replace the yogurt with Almond "Cream" (page 29) or coconut milk

Cherries, Banana, Buckwheat Porridge & Almonds

INGREDIENTS

⅓ cup buckwheat porridge made with almond milk
  (page 16)
1 banana, chopped
handful of cherries, pitted and halved
2 tbsp almonds

Strawberries, Banana, Cornflakes & Hazelnuts

INGREDIENTS

handful of cornflakes
handful of strawberries, chopped
1 banana, sliced
handful of hazelnuts
⅓ cup milk

VEGAN ALTERNATIVE

Replace the dairy milk with almond milk

Kiwi, Strawberries, Oats & Almonds

INGREDIENTS

⅓ cup oats, soaked overnight in ⅓ cup apple juice
handful of strawberries, chopped
1 kiwi, chopped
1½ tbsp almonds, chopped

VEGETARIAN ALTERNATIVE

Add ⅓ cup natural yogurt

VEGAN

Raspberries, Apricot, Quinoa Porridge & Cashews

INGREDIENTS

⅓ cup quinoa porridge made with almond milk (page 16)
2 small apricots, chopped
handful of raspberries
handful of cashew nuts

VEGETARIAN SAVOURY ALTERNATIVE

Replace the cashew nuts with 50 g [2 oz] goat cheese or ricotta cheese

Nectarine, Strawberries, Banana & Hazelnuts

INGREDIENTS

Banana and Lemon Mash (page 26)
1 nectarine, chopped
handful of strawberries, chopped
handful of hazelnuts, ground to a powder in a food processor

RAW

Strawberries, Pear Oats & Pistachios

INGREDIENTS

⅓ cup oats, soaked overnight in ⅓ cup almond milk
1 small pear, chopped
handful of strawberries, chopped
1 tbsp pistachios
edible viola flowers (optional)

VEGETARIAN ALTERNATIVE

Replace the almond milk with dairy milk

Blackcurrants, Clementine, Bran Flakes & Walnuts

INGREDIENTS

⅓ cup bran flakes
2 tbsp natural yogurt
segments from 1 clementine
handful of blackcurrants
handful of walnuts, chopped
1 tbsp goji berries, soaked in water for a few minutes

45

Blueberries, Strawberries, Cereal & Hemp Seeds

INGREDIENTS

½ cup gluten-free cereal flakes
⅓ cup almond milk
handful of strawberries, chopped
handful of blueberries
1 tbsp shelled hemp seeds

VEGETARIAN ALTERNATIVE

Replace the almond milk with dairy milk or natural yogurt

Strawberries, Cherries, Oats & Pine Nuts

VEGAN

INGREDIENTS

2 tbsp oats, soaked overnight in 2 tbsp coconut milk
handful of cherries, pitted and halved
handful of strawberries, chopped
2 tbsp pine nuts

VEGETARIAN ALTERNATIVE

Replace the coconut
milk with natural yogurt

Cherries, Red Grapefruit, Bran Flakes & Pistachios

INGREDIENTS

⅓ cup bran flakes
handful of cherries, pitted and halved
½ red grapefruit, cut into segments, plus any juice
2 tbsp pistachios

VEGETARIAN ALTERNATIVE

Add 2 tbsp single [light] cream or natural yogurt

Strawberries, Apricot, Couscous & Pine Nuts

INGREDIENTS

50 g [⅓ cup] couscous, cooked
2 small apricots, chopped
handful of strawberries, chopped
1 tbsp pine nuts
handful of fresh mint
1 edible calendula flower (optional)

OMNIVORE SAVOURY ALTERNATIVE

Add 30 g [1 oz] Parma
or smoked ham

49

Cherries, Raspberries, Quinoa & Sesame Seeds

INGREDIENTS

⅓ cup roasted quinoa (e.g. Qnola)
handful of cherries, pitted and halved
handful of raspberries
1 tbsp black sesame seeds
⅓ cup Almond "Cream" (page 29)
1 tsp flaked [slivered] almonds

VEGETARIAN ALTERNATIVE

Replace the Almond "Cream" with single [light] cream or milk

Cherries, Apricot, Cereal & Chia Seeds

INGREDIENTS

1 tbsp gluten-free cereal flakes
2 tbsp almond milk
handful of cherries, pitted and halved
2 apricots, chopped
1 tsp chia seeds

VEGETARIAN ALTERNATIVE

Replace the almond milk with natural yogurt

Raspberries, Nectarine, Porridge & Sesame Seeds

INGREDIENTS

⅓ cup amaranth porridge made with water (page 16)
1 nectarine, chopped
handful of raspberries
1 tsp black sesame seeds

OMNIVORE
SAVOURY
ALTERNATIVE

Add 30 g [1 oz] coppa
ham or bresaola

Apricot, Nectarine, Oats & Hemp Seeds

INGREDIENTS

1 tbsp oats, soaked overnight in 3 tbsp natural yogurt
2 apricots, chopped
1 nectarine, chopped
1 tbsp natural yogurt
1 tbsp shelled hemp seeds

RAW ALTERNATIVE

Replace the natural yogurt with Cashew "Cream" (page 29)

Raspberries, Blackcurrants, Rye Bread & Pistachios

INGREDIENTS

1 slice of rye bread, cut into strips
handful of raspberries
handful of blackcurrants
2 tbsp natural yogurt
1 tbsp pistachios

VEGETARIAN SAVOURY ALTERNATIVE

Replace the natural yogurt with cottage cheese, ricotta or even goat cheese

Blackcurrants, Kiwi, Cornflakes & Hemp Seeds

INGREDIENTS

⅓ cup cornflakes
⅓ cup almond milk
handful of blackcurrants
1 kiwi, chopped
1 tbsp shelled hemp seeds

VEGETARIAN ALTERNATIVE

Replace the almond milk with dairy milk

Mango, Raspberries Cereal & Yogurt

INGREDIENTS

⅓ cup cereal flakes
handful of raspberries
⅓ mango, chopped
2 tbsp natural yogurt
1 tsp poppy seeds

VEGAN ALTERNATIVE

Replace the natural yogurt with coconut yogurt or Cashew "Cream" (page 29)

Blackcurrants, Papaya, Rye Bread & Cashews

INGREDIENTS

½ papaya, deseeded and chopped
handful of blackcurrants
1 slice of rye bread, cut into strips
⅓ cup coconut yogurt
2 tbsp cashew nuts

RAW ALTERNATIVE

Replace the yogurt
with Cashew "Yogurt"
(page 29), and bread
with soaked oats

Raspberries, Apple, Cornflakes & Pistachios

INGREDIENTS

⅓ cup cornflakes
Banana and Lemon Mash (page 26)
1 small apple, chopped
handful of raspberries
1 tbsp pistachios

VEGETARIAN ALTERNATIVE

Add 1 tbsp natural yogurt

Blueberries, Watermelon, Bran Flakes & Pistachios

INGREDIENTS

⅓ cup bran flakes
1 small wedge of watermelon, deseeded and chopped
handful of blueberries
⅓ cup oat porridge made with almond milk (page 16)
1 tbsp pistachios

VEGETARIAN SAVOURY ALTERNATIVE

Replace the almond milk with water, and add 30 g [1 oz] feta cheese

Papaya, Pineapple, Quinoa & Pumpkin Seeds

INGREDIENTS

⅓ cup roasted quinoa (e.g. Qnola)

½ papaya, deseeded and chopped

1 small wedge of pineapple, chopped

2 tbsp hemp sour cream (made from blending 2 tbsp shelled hemp seeds, 1 tbsp lemon juice and 1 tbsp water)

1 tbsp pumpkin seeds

VEGETARIAN ALTERNATIVE

Replace the hemp sour cream with natural yogurt

White Grapefruit, Papaya, Couscous & Pistachios

INGREDIENTS

50 g [⅓ cup] couscous, cooked
½ papaya, deseeded and chopped
½ white grapefruit, chopped
1 tbsp pistachios
1 tsp dried rose petals
1 tsp bee pollen

Blackcurrants, Melon, Oats & Hemp Seeds

INGREDIENTS

*⅓ cup oats, soaked overnight in ⅓ cup almond milk
    and 1 tsp almond butter*
1 wedge of cantaloupe melon, chopped
handful of blackcurrants
1 tbsp shelled hemp seeds

VEGETARIAN ALTERNATIVE
Add 2 tbsp crème fraîche

Pineapple, Blueberries, Cereal & Pistachios

INGREDIENTS

⅓ cup gluten-free cereal flakes
1 small wedge of pineapple, chopped
handful of blueberries
2 tbsp natural yogurt
1 tbsp pistachios

VEGAN ALTERNATIVE

Replace the natural yogurt with Banana and Lemon Mash (page 26)

Watermelon, Apricot, Bran Flakes & Chia Seeds

INGREDIENTS

⅓ cup bran flakes
1 small wedge of watermelon, deseeded and chopped
1 apricot, chopped
2 tbsp natural yogurt
1 tsp chia seeds

VEGAN ALTERNATIVE

Replace the natural yogurt with Cashew "Yogurt" (page 29)

Strawberries, Melon, Cornflakes & Cashew "Yogurt"

INGREDIENTS

1/3 cup cornflakes
handful of strawberries, chopped
1 wedge of galia melon, chopped
2 tbsp Cashew "Yogurt" (page 29)
1 tsp poppy seeds

VEGETARIAN ALTERNATIVE

Replace the Cashew "Yogurt" with natural yogurt

Kiwi, Watermelon, Rice Granola & Pumpkin Seeds

INGREDIENTS

1 kiwi, chopped
1 small wedge of watermelon, deseeded and chopped
2 tbsp puffed rice granola
2 tbsp Almond "Cream" (page 29)
1 tsp pumpkin seeds

RAW ALTERNATIVE

Replace the puffed rice granola with 2 tbsp oats soaked in 2 tbsp almond milk

Fig, Strawberries, Cornflakes & Pistachios

INGREDIENTS

⅓ cup cornflakes
2 figs, chopped
handful of strawberries, chopped
2 tbsp natural yogurt
1 tbsp pistachios
edible viola flowers (optional)

Blackberries, Apricot, Oats & Linseeds

INGREDIENTS

⅓ cup oats, soaked overnight in ⅓ cup apple juice
handful of blackberries
3 small apricots, chopped
1 tsp linseeds

VEGETARIAN ALTERNATIVE

Add 1 tbsp crème fraîche

Papaya, Plum, Quinoa Porridge & Hemp Seeds

INGREDIENTS

⅓ cup quinoa porridge made with water (page 16)
½ papaya, deseeded and chopped
1 plum, chopped
1 tbsp shelled hemp seeds, ground to a powder in a food processor
handful of fresh mint
1 tbsp cocoa nibs

RAW ALTERNATIVE

Replace the quinoa porridge with ⅓ cup oats, soaked overnight in ⅓ cup apple juice

Melon, Watermelon, Oats & Hazelnuts

INGREDIENTS

⅓ cup oats, soaked overnight in ⅓ cup apple juice
   with 1 tsp ground ginger
1 small wedge of watermelon, deseeded and chopped
1 wedge of galia melon, chopped
handful of hazelnuts

VEGETARIAN
ALTERNATIVE
*Add 2 tbsp crème
fraîche*

Blackberries, Papaya, Porridge & Hemp Seeds

INGREDIENTS

⅓ cup buckwheat porridge made with water and
   1 tsp coconut oil (page 16)
½ papaya, deseeded and chopped
handful of blackberries
1 tbsp shelled hemp seeds

OMNIVORE SAVOURY ALTERNATIVE

Add 30 g [1 oz] Parma ham

Watermelon, Grapes, Oats & Hemp Seeds

INGREDIENTS

⅓ cup oats, soaked overnight in ⅓ cup almond milk with
   1 tsp ground cinnamon
1 small wedge of watermelon, deseeded and chopped
handful of red grapes
1 tbsp shelled hemp seeds

VEGETARIAN ALTERNATIVE

Add 2 tbsp crème fraîche

Physalis, Apple, Cornflakes & Hazelnuts

INGREDIENTS

2 tbsp cornflakes
½ apple, chopped
handful of physalis, skinned
2 tbsp Almond "Cream" (page 29)
1 tbsp hazelnuts
edible viola flowers (optional)

VEGETARIAN ALTERNATIVE

Replace the Almond "Cream" with dairy single [light] cream

Plum, Raspberries, Cereal & Pistachios

INGREDIENTS

2 tbsp gluten-free cereal flakes
1 plum, chopped
handful of raspberries
2 tbsp natural yogurt
1 tbsp pistachios

VEGAN ALTERNATIVE

Replace the natural yogurt with Cashew "Yogurt" (page 29)

Persimmon, Raspberries, Oats & Pumpkin Seeds

INGREDIENTS

⅓ cup oats, soaked overnight in ⅓ cup almond milk
handful of raspberries
1 small persimmon, cut into wedges
1 tbsp pumpkin seeds

**OMNIVORE
SAVOURY
ALTERNATIVE**

*Add 30 g [1 oz] cured
chorizo or smoked ham*

Watermelon, Blackberries, Bran Flakes & Cashews

INGREDIENTS

⅓ cup bran flakes
handful of blackberries
1 wedge of watermelon, deseeded and chopped, plus any juice
2 tbsp cashew nuts

Pomegranate, Plums, Bran Flakes & Chia Seeds

INGREDIENTS

1 tbsp bran flakes
2 plums, chopped
handful of pomegranate seeds
2 tbsp Almond "Cream" (page 29)
1 tsp chia seeds
handful of fresh tarragon

RAW ALTERNATIVE

Replace the bran flakes with oats soaked overnight in the Almond "Cream"

Blackberries, Melon, Oats & Chia Seeds

INGREDIENTS

⅓ cup oats, soaked overnight in ⅓ cup apple juice
handful of blackberries
1 wedge of galia melon, chopped
1 tsp chia seeds
couple of fresh mint leaves

VEGAN ALTERNATIVE

Add 1 tbsp toasted flaked [slivered] almonds

Pomegranate, Grapes, Quinoa & Coconut Yogurt

INGREDIENTS

2 tbsp roasted quinoa (e.g. Qnola)
handful of red grapes
2 tbsp pomegranate seeds
2 tbsp coconut yogurt
handful of fresh mint

VEGETARIAN ALTERNATIVE

Replace the coconut yogurt with natural yogurt

Physalis, Plum, Cereal & Pistachios

INGREDIENTS

⅓ cup gluten-free cereal flakes
handful of physalis, skinned
1 plum, chopped
2 tbsp natural yogurt
1 tbsp pistachios

VEGAN ALTERNATIVE

Replace the natural yogurt with oat cream or Cashew "Yogurt" (page 29)

Watermelon, Plum, Cornflakes & Chia Seeds

INGREDIENTS

⅓ cup cornflakes
1 small wedge of watermelon, deseeded and chopped
1 plum, chopped
2 tbsp Cashew "Yogurt" (page 29)
1 tsp chia seeds

VEGETARIAN ALTERNATIVE

Replace the Cashew "Yogurt" with dairy single [light] cream

Fig, Raspberries, Bran Flakes & Yogurt

INGREDIENTS

⅓ cup bran flakes
2 figs, chopped
handful of raspberries
2 tbsp natural yogurt

**VEGETARIAN
SAVOURY ALTERNATIVE**
*Replace the yogurt with
cottage cheese and the
bran with rye bread*

Blackberries, Plum, Oats & Almonds

INGREDIENTS

⅓ cup oats, soaked overnight in ⅓ cup orange juice
handful of blackberries
1 plum, chopped
2 tbsp Cashew "Yogurt" (page 29)
2 tbsp almonds, soaked in water overnight

VEGETARIAN ALTERNATIVE

Replace the Cashew "Yogurt" with natural yogurt

83

Blackberries, Nectarine, Bran Flakes & Walnuts

INGREDIENTS

⅓ cup bran flakes
2 tbsp milk
1 nectarine, chopped
handful of blackberries
handful of walnuts

VEGAN ALTERNATIVE

Replace the dairy milk with coconut milk

Fig, Apple, Oats & Pumpkin Seeds

INGREDIENTS

⅓ cup oats, soaked overnight in ⅓ cup apple juice
   with 1 tsp ground ginger
2 figs, chopped
½ apple, sliced
2 tbsp roasted quinoa (e.g. Qnola)
1 tsp dried coconut shavings
1 tsp pumpkin seeds

VEGETARIAN ALTERNATIVE

Replace the soaked oats with ⅓ cup porridge made with dairy milk (page 16)

Pomegranate, Melon, Cornflakes & Yogurt

INGREDIENTS

1 wedge of honeydew melon, chopped
2 tbsp pomegranate seeds
⅓ cup cornflakes
2 tbsp natural yogurt
edible viola flowers (optional)

VEGAN ALTERNATIVE

Replace the natural yogurt with Almond "Cream" (page 29) or oat cream

Fig, Pomegranate, Oats & Hemp Seeds

INGREDIENTS

⅓ cup oats, soaked overnight in ⅓ cup Almond "Cream"
   (page 29)
2 tbsp pomegranate seeds
2 figs, chopped
1 tbsp shelled hemp seeds

VEGAN ALTERNATIVE

Replace the Almond "Cream" with soy, oat or coconut milk

Apple, Coconut, Porridge & Chia Seeds

INGREDIENTS

*⅓ cup porridge made with almond milk (page 16)
and 1 tsp ground cinnamon
1 small apple, shaved with a vegetable peeler
flesh of ¼ fresh coconut, finely chopped
1 tsp chia seeds
½ teaspoon bee pollen*

Coconut, Banana, Oats & Hemp Seeds

INGREDIENTS

⅓ cup oats, soaked overnight in 3 tbsp natural yogurt
1 banana, sliced
flesh of ¼ fresh coconut, finely chopped
1 tbsp shelled hemp seeds
2 squares of dark chocolate, chopped

RAW ALTERNATIVE

Replace the yogurt with Almond "Cream" (page 29) and use raw dark chocolate chips

Watermelon, Orange & Pistachios

INGREDIENTS

2 tbsp Pistachio "Yogurt" (page 29)
1 small wedge of watermelon, deseeded and chopped
½ orange, chopped
1 tbsp pistachios
handful of fresh mint

VEGETARIAN ALTERNATIVE

Add 2 tbsp crème fraîche

Coconut, Blood Orange, Porridge & Hemp Seeds

INGREDIENTS

⅓ cup porridge made with almond milk (page 16) and
   1 tsp ground ginger
flesh of ¼ fresh coconut, chopped
½ blood orange, chopped
1 tbsp shelled hemp seeds

VEGETARIAN ALTERNATIVE

Replace the almond milk with dairy milk

Apple, Kiwi, Bran Flakes & Chia Seeds

INGREDIENTS

handful of bran flakes
Avocado Mash (page 27)
1 small apple, sliced
1 big kiwi, sliced
1 tsp chia seeds
½ teaspoon bee pollen and a handful of fresh mint

Coconut, Kiwi, Quinoa & Goji Berries

INGREDIENTS

50 g [⅓ cup] cooked black quinoa
flesh of ¼ fresh coconut, chopped
Banana and Lemon Mash (page 26)
1 kiwi, sliced
1 tbsp goji berries, soaked overnight in water

VEGETARIAN ALTERNATIVE

Replace the Banana and Lemon Mash with natural yogurt

Coconut, Papaya, Quinoa & Peanuts

INGREDIENTS

2 tbsp quinoa porridge made with water (page 16) and
   1 tsp ground ginger
flesh of ¼ fresh coconut, chopped
½ papaya, deseeded and chopped
2 tbsp peanuts, toasted
handful of fresh coriander [cilantro]

RAW ALTERNATIVE
Replace the quinoa porridge with oats soaked in coconut milk and don't toast the peanuts

Apple, Orange, Porridge & Chia Seeds

INGREDIENTS

⅓ cup porridge made with coconut milk (page 16)
   and 1 tsp ground turmeric
1 small apple, chopped
1 small orange, chopped
2 tbsp coconut yogurt
1 tsp chia seeds

VEGETARIAN ALTERNATIVE

Replace the coconut
yogurt with crème fraîche

Grapes, Apple, Oats & Hazelnuts

INGREDIENTS

⅓ cup oats, soaked overnight in ⅓ cup almond milk
   with 1 tsp ground cinnamon
1 small apple, chopped
handful of red grapes
handful of hazelnuts, chopped

VEGETARIAN ALTERNATIVE

Add 30 g [1 oz] soft,
fresh goat cheese

Red Grapefruit, Kiwi, Bran Flakes & Chia Seeds

INGREDIENTS

⅓ cup bran flakes
1 kiwi, chopped
½ red grapefruit, chopped
2 tbsp natural yogurt
1 tsp chia seeds

VEGAN ALTERNATIVE

Replace the natural yogurt with oat or soy cream

Banana, Grapefruit, Rye Bread & Cashew "Yogurt"

INGREDIENTS

3 tbsp Cashew "Yogurt" flavoured with raspberries
  (page 29)
1 slice of rye bread, chopped
1 banana, chopped
½ grapefruit, chopped
dried rose petals (optional) and handful of fresh mint

VEGETARIAN ALTERNATIVE

Replace the Cashew
"Yogurt" with raspberry
dairy yogurt

Pink Grapefruit, Avocado, Cereal & Pistachios

INGREDIENTS

handful of gluten-free cereal flakes
½ pink grapefruit, chopped
½ avocado, chopped
1 tbsp pistachios
1 tbsp Almond "Cream" (page 29)
edible pansies (optional)

VEGETARIAN ALTERNATIVE

Replace the Almond "Cream" with natural yogurt

Physalis, Pear, Oats & Poppy Seeds

INGREDIENTS

⅓ cup oats, soaked overnight in ⅓ cup natural yogurt
   and 2 tbsp apple juice
handful of physalis, skinned
½ pear, chopped
1 tsp poppy seeds

VEGAN
ALTERNATIVE

Replace the natural
yogurt with almond milk

Pomegranate, Banana, Granola & Bee Pollen

INGREDIENTS

⅓ cup granola
1 banana, sliced
2 tbsp pomegranate seeds
2 tbsp natural yogurt
1 tsp bee pollen

VEGAN ALTERNATIVE

Replace the yogurt with coconut yogurt or Cashew "Yogurt" (page 29) and omit the pollen

Banana, Kiwi, Quinoa & Sunflower Seeds

INGREDIENTS

2 tbsp coconut yogurt
1 banana, sliced
1 kiwi, chopped
1 tbsp roasted quinoa (e.g. Qnola)
1 tsp sunflower seeds
1 tsp dried coconut shavings

VEGETARIAN ALTERNATIVE

Replace the coconut yogurt with natural yogurt

Kiwi, Orange, Muesli & Bee Pollen

INGREDIENTS

2 tbsp muesli
1 kiwi, chopped
½ orange, chopped
2 tbsp natural yogurt
1 tsp goji berries, soaked in water for a few minutes
1 tsp bee pollen

VEGAN ALTERNATIVE

Replace the natural yogurt with Cashew "Yogurt" (page 29) and omit the bee pollen

Red Grapefruit, Mango, Bran Flakes & Chia Seeds

INGREDIENTS

2 tbsp bran flakes
½ small mango, chopped
½ red grapefruit, chopped, plus any juice
1 tsp chia seeds
handful of fresh mint

VEGETARIAN ALTERNATIVE

Add 2 or 3 tbsp natural yogurt or 30 g [1 oz] goat cheese

Persimmon, Apple, Porridge & Walnuts

INGREDIENTS

⅓ cup porridge made with dairy milk (page 16) and
   1 tsp ground cinnamon
½ persimmon, sliced
½ apple, shredded with a julienne peeler
2 tsp walnuts, ground to a powder in a food processor

VEGAN
ALTERNATIVE
Replace the dairy
milk with coconut milk

Pink Grapefruit, Apple, Banana & Hemp Seeds

INGREDIENTS

Banana and Lemon Mash (page 26)
½ pink grapefruit, chopped
½ apple, chopped
1 tbsp shelled hemp seeds

VEGAN ALTERNATIVE

Add 2 tbsp coconut yogurt

Plum, Grapes, Cornflakes & Chia Seeds

INGREDIENTS

Banana and Lemon Mash (page 26)
⅓ cup cornflakes
2 small plums, chopped
handful of red grapes
1 tsp chia seeds
a few fresh mint leaves and 1 edible pansy (optional)

RAW ALTERNATIVE

Replace the cornflakes with ⅓ cup oats, soaked overnight in ⅓ cup orange juice

Pear, Grapefruit, Oats & Goji Berries

INGREDIENTS

⅓ cup oats, soaked overnight in ⅓ cup orange juice
½ pear, chopped
½ grapefruit, chopped
1 tbsp goji berries, soaked in water for a few minutes
1 tsp black sesame seeds
1 tsp raw honey

VEGETARIAN
ALTERNATIVE
*Add 1 tbsp natural
yogurt*

Pear, Plum, Oats & Bee Pollen

INGREDIENTS

2 tbsp oats, soaked overnight in 3 tbsp natural yogurt
    with 1 tsp ground ginger
½ pear, chopped
2 plums, chopped
1 tsp bee pollen
1 tsp poppy seeds

VEGAN ALTERNATIVE

Omit the bee pollen and replace the natural yogurt with oat or soy cream

Apple, Pomegranate, Couscous & Pumpkin Seeds

INGREDIENTS

50 g [⅓ cup] couscous, cooked
1 small apple, chopped
2 tbsp pomegranate seeds
2 tbsp natural yogurt
1 tbsp pumpkin seeds
sprig of fresh mint

VEGAN ALTERNATIVE

Replace the natural yogurt with coconut yogurt or Cashew "Yogurt" (page 29)

Pear, Kiwi, Quinoa & Linseeds

INGREDIENTS

50 g [⅓ cup] black quinoa, cooked
½ pear, chopped
1 kiwi, chopped
1 tbsp goji berries, soaked in water for a few minutes
handful of fresh mint
1 tsp linseeds

RAW ALTERNATIVE

Replace the quinoa
with ⅓ cup oats, soaked
overnight in ⅓ cup
apple juice

VEGAN

Passion Fruit, Kiwi, Bran Flakes & Hemp Seeds

INGREDIENTS

⅓ cup bran flakes
seeds from 1 passion fruit
1 kiwi, sliced
2 tbsp oat or soy single [light] cream
1 tbsp shelled hemp seeds

RAW ALTERNATIVE

Replace the cream with Almond "Cream" (page 29) and replace the bran with oats soaked in juice

Kiwi, Pomegranate, Rye Bread & Walnuts

INGREDIENTS

1 slice of rye bread, chopped
2 tbsp natural yogurt
2 tbsp pomegranate seeds
1 kiwi, sliced
handful of walnuts

Orange, Pear, Buckwheat & Walnuts

INGREDIENTS

50 g [⅓ cup] buckwheat, cooked
½ pear, chopped
½ orange, chopped
handful of fresh mint, chopped
1 tsp black sesame seeds
2 tbsp walnuts

RAW ALTERNATIVE

Replace the buckwheat with ⅓ cup oats, soaked overnight in ⅓ cup orange juice

Pomegranate, Orange, Couscous & Pistachios

VEGAN

INGREDIENTS

50 g [⅓ cup] couscous, cooked
1 small orange, chopped
2 tbsp pomegranate seeds
1 tbsp pistachios
handful of prunes, pitted

VEGETARIAN ALTERNATIVE

Add 1 tbsp natural yogurt

Pomegranate, Pineapple, Oats & Chia Seeds

INGREDIENTS

1 tbsp chia seeds and 1 tbsp oats, soaked for
    a few minutes in ⅓ cup almond milk
1 small wedge of pineapple, chopped
2 tbsp pomegranate seeds
1 tsp chia seeds
handful of fresh mint

VEGETARIAN ALTERNATIVE

*Add 2 tbsp crème
fraîche*

Passion Fruit, Banana, Quinoa & Cashews

VEGAN

INGREDIENTS

50 g [⅓ cup] black quinoa, cooked
1 banana, chopped
seeds from 1 passion fruit
handful of fresh basil mint, or mint
1 tbsp cashew nuts

VEGETARIAN ALTERNATIVE

Add 2 tbsp crème fraîche

Lychee, Kiwi, Porridge & Chia Seeds

INGREDIENTS

⅓ cup porridge made with coconut milk (page 16)
   and 1 tsp ground ginger
4 lychees, pitted and halved
1 kiwi, chopped
1 tsp chia seeds
1 tbsp goji berries, soaked in water for a few minutes

RAW ALTERNATIVE

Replace the milk with almond milk and soak the oats overnight instead of cooking them

Pineapple, Coconut, Quinoa & Pistachios

INGREDIENTS

Banana and Lemon Mash (page 26)
1 small wedge of pineapple, chopped
flesh of ¼ fresh coconut, chopped
1 tbsp pistachios
1 tbsp roasted quinoa (e.g. Qnola)

RAW ALTERNATIVE

Replace the quinoa
with 1 tbsp shelled
hemp seeds

Pomegranate, Papaya, Rye Bread & Bee Pollen

INGREDIENTS

1 slice of rye bread, cut into cubes
½ papaya, chopped
2 tbsp pomegranate seeds
2 tbsp natural yogurt
1 tsp bee pollen

VEGAN ALTERNATIVE

Replace the natural yogurt with oat or soy cream, and omit the pollen

Passion Fruit, Apple, Banana & Açai Berries

INGREDIENTS

1 banana, blended with 50 g [1/3 cup] frozen açai berries
1/2 apple, finely chopped
seeds from 1 passion fruit
1 tsp bee pollen
1 tbsp cashew nuts

VEGAN
ALTERNATIVE
Omit the bee pollen

Persimmon, Red Grapefruit, Oats & Chia Seeds

INGREDIENTS

⅓ cup oats, soaked overnight in 2 tbsp almond milk
½ ripe persimmon, chopped
½ red grapefruit, chopped
1 tsp chia seeds
1 tsp pared orange zest
1 tsp raw honey

VEGAN ALTERNATIVE

Add 2 tbsp coconut yogurt and omit the honey

Lychee, Pear, Cornflakes & Hazelnuts

INGREDIENTS

⅓ cup cornflakes
1 pear, chopped
4 lychees, pitted and halved
2 tbsp hazelnuts
handful of fresh mint

VEGETARIAN ALTERNATIVE

Add 1 tbsp single [light] cream or whipped cream

Mango, Apple, Quinoa & Yogurt

INGREDIENTS

50 g [⅓ cup] black quinoa, cooked
2 tbsp natural yogurt
½ mango, chopped
½ apple, shredded with a julienne peeler

VEGAN ALTERNATIVE

Replace the natural yogurt with Cashew "Cream" (page 29)

Mango, Passion Fruit, Cornflakes & Poppy Seeds

INGREDIENTS

Banana and Lemon Mash (page 26)
⅓ cup cornflakes
seeds from 1 passion fruit
2 tbsp dried coconut shavings
½ mango, chopped
1 tsp poppy seeds

Lychee, Blood Orange, Oats & Hemp Seeds

VEGAN

INGREDIENTS

⅓ cup oats, soaked overnight in ⅓ cup blood orange juice
  and 1 tsp ground ginger
4 lychees, pitted and halved
1 blood orange, chopped
handful of fresh mint
1 tbsp shelled hemp seeds

VEGETARIAN ALTERNATIVE
Add 1 tbsp single [light] cream or whipped cream

Lychee, Pineapple, Oats & Walnuts

INGREDIENTS

⅓ cup oats, soaked overnight in 2 tbsp natural yogurt
   and 1 tsp ground ginger
4 lychees, pitted and chopped
1 small wedge of pineapple, chopped
1 tbsp walnuts, ground to a powder in a food processor
handful of fresh mint

RAW ALTERNATIVE

Replace the natural yogurt with Cashew "Yogurt" (page 29)

Mango, Coconut, Bran Flakes & Goji Berries

INGREDIENTS

2 tbsp bran flakes
3 tbsp soy or oat cream
flesh of ¼ fresh coconut, chopped
½ mango, chopped
1 tbsp goji berries, soaked in water for a few minutes

**VEGETARIAN
ALTERNATIVE**

*Replace the soy cream
with natural yogurt*

Avocado, Coconut, Bran Flakes & Chia Seeds

INGREDIENTS

⅓ cup bran flakes
2 tbsp roasted quinoa (e.g. Qnola)
2 tbsp natural yogurt mixed with seeds from 1 passion fruit
½ avocado, chopped
handful of dried coconut shavings
1 tsp chia seeds

VEGAN ALTERNATIVE

Replace the natural yogurt with coconut yogurt

Savoury

Plum, Melon, Buckwheat & Goat Cheese

INGREDIENTS

50 g [⅓ cup] buckwheat, cooked
1 wedge of cantaloupe or honeydew melon, chopped
1 red plum, chopped
30 g [¼ cup] chopped goat cheese
handful of fresh mint, chopped
a drizzle of extra virgin cold-pressed rapeseed [canola] oil

OMNIVORE ALTERNATIVE

Add 2 slices of Parma ham

Pear, Grapes, Rye Bread & Blue Cheese

INGREDIENTS

1 small pear, chopped
handful of red grapes
30 g [¼ cup] chopped blue cheese
1 slice of rye bread, cut into strips
handful of walnuts

OMNIVORE ALTERNATIVE

Replace the cheese with
coppa or speck ham

Blackberries, Fig, Rye Bread & Goat Cheese

INGREDIENTS

2 figs, chopped
handful of blackberries
30 g [¼ cup] crumbled goat cheese
handful of almonds, soaked overnight in water
1 slice of rye bread or toasted sourdough bread, torn
handful of fresh basil

VEGAN
ALTERNATIVE
Replace the goat cheese with Cashew "Cream" (page 29)

Melon, Fig, Rye Bread & Parma Ham

INGREDIENTS

1 slice of rye bread, cut into strips
1 wedge of galia or honeydew melon, chopped
2 figs, chopped
2 slices of Parma ham, cut into strips
a drizzle of extra virgin cold-pressed rapeseed [canola] oil

Physalis, Grapes, Couscous & Ricotta Salata

INGREDIENTS

50 g [⅓ cup] couscous, cooked
handful of physalis, skinned
handful of red grapes
handful of walnuts
30 g [¼ cup] chopped ricotta salata
a drizzle of extra virgin cold-pressed rapeseed [canola] oil

VEGAN ALTERNATIVE

Replace the ricotta salata with 2 tbsp Cashew "Yogurt" (page 29)

Nectarine, Fig, Sourdough Bread & Goat Cheese

INGREDIENTS

1 white nectarine, chopped
2 figs, chopped
30 g [¼ cup] chopped goat cheese
small handful of walnuts, chopped
1 slice of sourdough bread, toasted and halved
a drizzle of extra virgin cold-pressed rapeseed [canola] oil

Raspberries, Blackberries, Rye Bread & Cheese

INGREDIENTS

1 slice of rye bread, chopped
handful of raspberries
handful of blackberries
2 tbsp cottage cheese
handful of walnuts, chopped
a drizzle of extra virgin cold-pressed rapeseed [canola] oil

VEGAN SWEET ALTERNATIVE

Replace the cottage cheese with coconut yogurt

Blackcurrants, Apricot, Couscous & Cheese

INGREDIENTS

50 g [⅓ cup] couscous, cooked
handful of blackcurrants
1 big apricot, chopped
2 tbsp cottage cheese
1 tbsp linseeds and 1 edible nasturtium flower (optional)
a drizzle of extra virgin cold-pressed rapeseed [canola] oil

VEGAN
SWEET ALTERNATIVE
Replace the cottage cheese with Almond "Yogurt" (page 29)

Pomegranate, Pear, Porridge & Ricotta

VEGETARIAN

INGREDIENTS

1 small pear, chopped
seeds from ½ pomegranate
½ cup porridge made with water and a pinch of salt
   (page 16)
50 g [¼ cup] ricotta cheese
1 tsp chia seeds and 1 edible pansy (optional)

RAW ALTERNATIVE

Replace the cheese with
Cashew "Yogurt" (page 29)
and the porridge with oats
soaked in almond
milk

Raspberries, Grapes, Quinoa & Ricotta Salata

INGREDIENTS

50 g [⅓ cup] quinoa, cooked
handful of raspberries
handful of black grapes
30 g [¼ cup] shaved ricotta salata, using a vegetable peeler
handful of cashew nuts
a drizzle of extra virgin cold-pressed rapeseed [canola] oil

VEGAN

Pomegranate, Avocado, Quinoa & Sesame Seeds

INGREDIENTS

80 g [½ cup] quinoa, cooked
½ avocado, chopped
seeds from ½ pomegranate
1 tsp black and white sesame seeds
a few edible calendula petals (optional)

VEGETARIAN ALTERNATIVE

Add 30 g [¼ cup] chopped Manchego or goat cheese

Aubergine, Courgette, Barley & Feta

INGREDIENTS

45 g [¼ cup] pearl barley, cooked
½ aubergine [eggplant], chopped and roasted
1 courgette [zucchini], chopped and roasted
30 g [¼ cup] chopped feta cheese
handful of fresh parsley

OMNIVORE ALTERNATIVE

Add 30 g [1 oz] cured chorizo or smoked ham

Blackberries, Grapes, Rye Bread & Parma Ham

INGREDIENTS

handful of blackberries
handful of red grapes
2 slices of Parma or coppa ham, torn into strips
1 slice of rye bread, cut into strips
1 tbsp pine nuts, toasted

VEGETARIAN ALTERNATIVE

Replace the ham with 30 g [¼ cup] chopped goat cheese

Blueberries, Avocado, Rye Bread & Goat Cheese

INGREDIENTS

1 avocado, chopped
handful of blueberries
30 g [¼ cup] chopped goat cheese
1 slice of rye bread, cut into strips

VEGAN SWEET ALTERNATIVE

Replace the cheese with 2 tbsp Cashew "Cream" (page 29) or nut butter

VEGAN

Aubergine, Avocado, Porridge & Sesame Seeds

INGREDIENTS

¼ cup porridge made with coconut milk (page 16)
½ aubergine [eggplant], chopped and roasted
½ avocado, chopped
1 tsp black sesame seeds
handful of fresh coriander [cilantro]
a sprinkle of dried chilli [red pepper] flakes

**OMNIVORE
ALTERNATIVE**
Add 30 g [1 oz]
roasted chicken or peeled,
cooked sustainable
prawns [shrimp]

Pomegranate, Aubergine, Brown Rice & Sesame Seeds

INGREDIENTS

50 g [¼ cup] brown rice, cooked
40 g [¼ cup] green or Puy lentils, cooked
1 tsp toasted sesame oil
½ aubergine [eggplant], chopped and roasted
seeds from ½ pomegranate
1 tsp sesame seeds

VEGETARIAN ALTERNATIVE

Add 1 tbsp labneh or Greek yogurt

Blood Orange, Avocado, Brown Rice & Shrimp

INGREDIENTS

50 g [¼ cup] brown rice, cooked
½ blood orange, deseeded and chopped
½ avocado, chopped
10–12 peeled, cooked sustainable prawns [small shrimp]
handful of fresh coriander [cilantro]
a drizzle of extra virgin cold-pressed rapeseed [canola] oil

VEGAN ALTERNATIVE

Replace the prawns [shrimp] with a handful of cashew nuts

Cucumber, Avocado, Rice Porridge & Smoked Salmon

INGREDIENTS

¼ cup rice porridge made with water (page 16)

50 g [2 oz] cucumber, peeled and chopped

½ avocado, chopped

2 slices of smoked salmon, torn

1 tsp sesame seeds, toasted

1 tsp dried dulse seaweed sprinkles

VEGETARIAN ALTERNATIVE

Replace the smoked salmon with a poached or hard-boiled egg

Carrot, Olives, Amaranth & Goat Cheese

INGREDIENTS

50 g [¼ cup] amaranth, cooked
1 carrot, shaved with a vegetable peeler
handful of black olives, pitted
40 g [¼ cup] crumbled goat cheese
handful of fresh mint
1 tbsp pistachios

PESCATARIAN ALTERNATIVE

Add 50 g [2 oz] poached cod or trout

Aubergine, Pepper, Brown Rice & Pistachios

INGREDIENTS

50 g [¼ cup] brown rice, cooked
¼ aubergine [eggplant], chopped and roasted
½ red and ½ yellow [bell] pepper, chopped and roasted
2 tbsp natural yogurt
1 tbsp pistachios

OMNIVORE ALTERNATIVE

Add a couple of small chunks of poached chicken

Mushroom, Courgette, Beans & Pancetta

INGREDIENTS

½ courgette [zucchini], julienned or shaved
50 g [1 cup] brown mushrooms, chopped and roasted
2 tbsp canned black-eyed beans
30 g [1 oz] pancetta, fried
handful of fresh parsley
a drizzle of extra virgin cold-pressed olive oil

VEGAN ALTERNATIVE

Replace the pancetta
with 1 tbsp sesame seeds
and 1 tbsp hummus

Carrot, Tomato, Buckwheat & Sardine

INGREDIENTS

40 g [¼ cup] buckwheat, cooked
1 carrot, shaved with a vegetable peeler
handful of cherry tomatoes, halved
2 cooked sardines
handful of fresh parsley
½ avocado, mashed with 1 tbsp lemon juice and 1 tbsp oil
1 tsp black sesame seeds

Carrot, Pepper, Black Rice & Halloumi

INGREDIENTS

40 g [¼ cup] black rice, cooked
1 carrot, shaved with a vegetable peeler
½ red and ½ green [bell] pepper, chopped and roasted
30 g [¼ cup] chopped halloumi cheese, roasted

OMNIVORE ALTERNATIVE
Add 30 g [1 oz] cooked bacon or pancetta

Courgette, Green Beans, Rye Bread & Pine Nuts

INGREDIENTS

½ small courgette [zucchini], julienned or shaved
1 slice of rye bread, chopped
small handful of green beans, steamed
handful of pine nuts
a drizzle of extra virgin cold-pressed olive oil
a few fresh mint leaves

VEGETARIAN ALTERNATIVE

Add 2 tbsp ricotta or cottage cheese

Courgette, Tomato, Avocado & Hemp Seeds

INGREDIENTS

½ courgette [zucchini], shaved with a vegetable peeler
handful of cherry tomatoes, halved
handful of fresh coriander [cilantro]
½ avocado, mashed with 1 tbsp lemon juice and 1 tbsp oil
1 tsp shelled hemp seeds
a drizzle of extra virgin cold-pressed olive oil

OMNIVORE ALTERNATIVE
Add 30 g [1 oz]
Parma or smoked ham

Courgette, Mushroom, Buckwheat & Egg

INGREDIENTS

40 g [¼ cup] buckwheat, cooked
1 small courgette [zucchini], julienned, and 1 egg,
   fried together in a pan
50 g [1 cup] brown mushrooms, sliced and roasted
1 spring onion [scallion], chopped
handful of fresh mint and 1 edible nasturtium (optional)

VEGAN

Courgette, Pepper, Barley & Sesame Seeds

INGREDIENTS

½ courgette [zucchini], julienned
45 g [¼ cup] pearl barley, cooked
1 red [bell] pepper, sliced
1 tsp black sesame seeds
1 spring onion [scallion], chopped
a drizzle of extra virgin cold-pressed olive oil

PESCATARIAN ALTERNATIVE

Add a handful
of peeled, cooked
sustainable prawns
[shrimp]

Carrot, Cucumber, Rye Bread & Feta

INGREDIENTS

1 carrot, shaved with a vegetable peeler
100 g [3½ oz] cucumber, peeled and chopped
30 g [¼ cup] crumbled feta
1 slice of rye bread, cut into strips
1 tsp poppy seeds
handful of fresh basil

VEGAN ALTERNATIVE

Replace the feta with 50 g [⅓ cup] canned chickpeas [garbanzo beans], or hummus

Cucumber, Blueberries, Rye Bread & Linseeds

INGREDIENTS

50 g [2 oz] cucumber, chopped
handful of blueberries
2 tbsp natural yogurt
1 slice of rye or wholewheat bread, cut into strips
1 tsp linseeds
handful of fresh mint and 1 edible dandelion (optional)

VEGAN ALTERNATIVE

Replace the natural yogurt with Cashew "Yogurt" (page 29)

Blueberries, Fig, Rye Bread & Hazelnuts

INGREDIENTS

⅓ cup Almond "Cream" (page 29)
handful of blueberries
2 figs, chopped
1 slice of rye bread, cut into strips
2 tbsp hazelnuts
handful of fresh mint

VEGETARIAN ALTERNATIVE

Replace the Almond "Cream" with 30 g [¼ cup] chopped goat cheese

Cucumber, Olives, Croutons & Mackerel

INGREDIENTS

50 g [2 oz] cucumber, peeled and chopped
handful of black olives, pitted
½ smoked mackerel fillet
handful of croutons
handful of fresh parsley
a drizzle of extra virgin cold-pressed olive oil

VEGETARIAN ALTERNATIVE

Replace the mackerel with feta cheese or halloumi

Courgette, Squash, Millet & Lentils

INGREDIENTS

½ courgette [zucchini], shaved with a vegetable peeler

50 g [½ cup] chopped butternut squash, roasted

40 g [¼ cup] green or Puy lentils, cooked

handful of fresh mint

40 g [¼ cup] millet, cooked

a drizzle of extra virgin cold-pressed olive oil

Cucumber, Sun-Dried Tomato, Bread & Ham

INGREDIENTS

1 slice of rye or toasted wholewheat bread, chopped
50 g [2 oz] cucumber, peeled and chopped
handful of sun-dried tomatoes
30 g [1 oz] smoked ham, chopped
1 tsp black sesame seeds
handful of fresh chervil

VEGETARIAN ALTERNATIVE

Replace the ham with mozzarella or ricotta cheese

Cucumber, Tomato, Rye Bread & Halloumi

INGREDIENTS

50 g [2 oz] cucumber, peeled and chopped
handful of cherry tomatoes, halved
30 g [¼ cup] chopped halloumi, fried
1 slice of rye bread, cut into strips
1 tsp sesame seeds, toasted
a drizzle of extra virgin cold-pressed olive oil and fresh mint

VEGAN ALTERNATIVE

Replace the halloumi with 50 g [⅓ cup] canned chickpeas [garbanzo beans]

Pomegranate, Mushroom & Chickpeas

INGREDIENTS

50 g [¼ cup] amaranth, cooked
50 g [1 cup] brown mushrooms, chopped and fried
30 g [¼ cup] canned chickpeas [garbanzo beans]
seeds from ½ pomegranate
a few fresh basil leaves
a drizzle of extra virgin cold-pressed olive oil

VEGETARIAN ALTERNATIVE

Add 2 tbsp natural yogurt

Green Beans, Avocado, Rye Bread & Pancetta

INGREDIENTS

small handful of green beans, steamed

½ avocado, chopped

30 g [1 oz] pancetta, fried

1 slice of rye or toasted wholewheat bread, cut into strips

a drizzle of extra virgin cold-pressed olive oil

VEGETARIAN ALTERNATIVE

Replace the pancetta with halloumi

Tomato, Aubergine, Chickpeas & Sesame Seeds

INGREDIENTS

50 g [2 oz] aubergine [eggplant], chopped and roasted
handful of cherry tomatoes, halved
50 g [⅓ cup] canned chickpeas [garbanzo beans]
1 tsp sesame seeds
a few fresh parsley leaves
a drizzle of extra virgin cold-pressed olive oil

OMNIVORE ALTERNATIVE

Add 30 g [1 oz] cured chorizo or smoked ham

Green Beans, Aubergine, Quinoa & Pecorino

INGREDIENTS

40 g [¼ cup] quinoa, cooked
½ small aubergine [eggplant], chopped and roasted
small handful of green beans, steamed
30 g [¼ cup] crumbled Pecorino
a drizzle of extra virgin cold-pressed olive oil

Green Beans, Squash, Buckwheat & Manchego

INGREDIENTS

40 g [¼ cup] buckwheat, cooked
50 g [½ cup] chopped butternut squash, roasted
small handful of green beans, steamed
30 g [¼ cup] chopped Manchego
sprig of fresh basil
a drizzle of extra virgin cold-pressed olive oil

OMNIVORE ALTERNATIVE

Replace the Manchego with roasted chicken

Mushroom, Green Beans, Rice & Egg

INGREDIENTS

40 g [¼ cup] black rice, cooked
50 g [1 cup] shiitake mushrooms, sliced and fried
small handful of green beans, steamed
½ avocado, chopped
1 fried egg
1 tsp sesame seeds, toasted

OMNIVORE ALTERNATIVE

Replace the egg with
30 g [1 oz] roasted
chicken

Pepper, Cucumber, Brown Rice & Tuna

INGREDIENTS

50 g [¼ cup] brown rice, cooked
50 g [2 oz] cucumber, peeled and chopped
½ red [bell] pepper, sliced
30 g [1 oz] canned tuna, broken into pieces
1 tsp dried nori seaweed flakes and 1 tsp poppy seeds
a drizzle of extra virgin cold-pressed olive oil

VEGETARIAN ALTERNATIVE

Replace the tuna with feta or halloumi

Mushroom, Squash, Buckwheat & Sesame Seeds

INGREDIENTS

40 g [¼ cup] buckwheat, cooked
50 g [½ cup] chopped butternut squash, roasted
50 g [1 cup] oyster mushrooms, sliced and fried
1 tsp sesame seeds, toasted
a few fresh basil leaves
a drizzle of extra virgin cold-pressed olive oil

VEGETARIAN ALTERNATIVE

Add 1 poached or hard-boiled egg

Tomato, Green Beans, Bread & Ricotta

INGREDIENTS

3 cherry tomatoes, chopped
small handful of green beans, steamed
2 tbsp ricotta
1 slice of toasted bread, halved
2 tbsp pine nuts

Mushroom, Avocado, Buckwheat & Egg

INGREDIENTS

40 g [¼ cup] buckwheat, cooked
½ avocado, chopped
50 g [1 cup] brown mushrooms, sliced and fried
1 hard-boiled egg, halved
1 tsp black sesame seeds
a drizzle of extra virgin cold-pressed olive oil

VEGAN ALTERNATIVE

Replace the egg with 2 tbsp canned chickpeas [garbanzo beans] or steamed edamame beans

Tomato, Avocado, Rye Bread & Bresaola

INGREDIENTS

handful of cherry tomatoes, chopped
handful of black kalamata olives, pitted and chopped
½ avocado, sliced
50 g [2 oz] bresaola, torn
1 slice of rye bread, cut into strips
a drizzle of extra virgin cold-pressed olive oil

Courgette, Olive, Beans & Mackerel

INGREDIENTS

½ courgette [zucchini], julienned or shaved
handful of black olives, pitted
2 tbsp cooked black-eyed beans
1 smoked mackerel fillet, shredded
handful of fresh parsley
a drizzle of extra virgin cold-pressed olive oil

Olive, Pepper, Quinoa & Feta

INGREDIENTS

40 g [¼ cup] quinoa, cooked
handful of black olives, pitted
½ red and ½ yellow [bell] pepper, chopped and roasted
30 g [¼ cup] crumbled feta cheese
handful of fresh basil
a drizzle of extra virgin cold-pressed olive oil

OMNIVORE
ALTERNATIVE

*Add 30 g [1 oz]
roasted chicken or cured
chorizo*

Squash, Pepper, Quinoa & Feta

INGREDIENTS

40 g [¼ cup] red quinoa, cooked
50 g [½ cup] chopped butternut squash, roasted
1 red [bell] pepper, chopped and roasted
30 g [¼ cup] chopped feta
handful of fresh basil mint, or mint
a drizzle of extra virgin cold-pressed olive oil

Tomato, Avocado, Rice & Omelette

INGREDIENTS

3 cherry tomatoes, roasted
½ avocado, chopped
1 small omelette
60 g [⅓ cup] white rice, cooked
handful of fresh coriander [cilantro]

Pepper, Green Beans, Barley & Walnuts

INGREDIENTS

45 g [¼ cup] pearl barley, cooked
small handful of green beans, steamed
½ red [bell] pepper, sliced
handful of walnuts
a drizzle of extra virgin cold-pressed olive oil
a few edible calendula petals (optional)

VEGETARIAN ALTERNATIVE

Add 30 g [¼ cup] chopped Manchego cheese

Pepper, Cucumber, Rye Bread & Hummus

INGREDIENTS

50 g [2 oz] cucumber, peeled and chopped
½ red [bell] pepper, chopped
1 slice of rye bread, cut into strips
2 tbsp hummus
1 tsp linseeds, toasted
fresh parsley and a drizzle of extra virgin cold-pressed olive oil

OMNIVORE ALTERNATIVE
Add 30 g [1 oz]
Parma ham or bresaola

Pomegranate, Squash, Black Rice & Yogurt

INGREDIENTS

40 g [¼ cup] black rice, coooked
50 g [½ cup] chopped butternut squash, roasted
seeds from ½ pomegranate
2 tbsp natural yogurt
1 tsp pine nuts
a drizzle of extra virgin cold-pressed olive oil

Squash, Olive, Amaranth & Smoked Ham

INGREDIENTS

50 g [¼ cup] amaranth, cooked
50 g [½ cup] chopped butternut squash, roasted
handful of kalamata olives, pitted and halved
30 g [1 oz] smoked ham, shredded
handful of fresh mint
a drizzle of extra virgin cold-pressed olive oil

PESCATARIAN ALTERNATIVE

Replace the smoked ham with smoked mackerel

Tomato, Mushroom, Rye Bread & Cannellini Beans

INGREDIENTS

handful of cherry tomatoes, fried
50 g [1 cup] brown mushrooms, sliced and fried
50 g [⅓ cup] canned cannellini beans, fried
1 slice of rye or toasted wholewheat bread, cut into strips
handful of fresh parsley
a drizzle of extra virgin cold-pressed olive oil

VEGETARIAN ALTERNATIVE
Add 30 g [1 oz] mozzarella or 1 hard-boiled egg

Olive, Avocado, Quinoa & Hemp Seeds

INGREDIENTS

40 g [¼ cup] red quinoa, cooked
½ avocado, chopped
handful of black olives, pitted
1 tbsp shelled hemp seeds
handful of fresh coriander [cilantro]
a drizzle of extra virgin cold-pressed olive oil

VEGETARIAN ALTERNATIVE
Add 2 tbsp ricotta or cottage cheese

Pepper, Avocado, Quinoa & Omelette

INGREDIENTS

40 g [¼ cup] black quinoa, cooked
1 red [bell] pepper, sliced and roasted
½ avocado, chopped
1 small omelette
handful of fresh tarragon
a drizzle of extra virgin cold-pressed olive oil

Index

Acknowledgments

I thank my wife and my son, who always make my life so rich. I thank my family, as they are always there to support me – my dad, aunt and uncle; they are wonderful!

I thank my extended family in Pesaro and Mirandola who always show a lot of love and affection and treat me like a son.

I thank my editor Céline and agent Claudia for believing in this second adventure. I also thank all the people at Quadrille for the fantastic work they did on *Salad Love*.

I thank all my friends who support me in life and follow my journey through social media; they are my second voice.

I thank all my followers and supporters who give me so much affection and encouragement to continue my work.